This WORKBOOK belongs to an incredible CREATOR of DREAMS come true...

Name:

Contact Details:

DRAW OR
Add a photo
of you

DEDICATION

to DAWSY + our 2 MERMAIDS + ouR PROMISE to CREATE an Amazing life together ♥ ♥ ♥

PHiLanTHROPy is ♥ iN AcTion

A PoRTion of PRofits fRoM EVERY book is RE-DiRected to AusTRALIAN WiLDLiFE CONSERVANCY

Book Deets

HEy. ThANK YOu foR BEiNG BORN ♥ ThANK You foR Being You! ♥ Me

CONTENTS!

MUST HAVE ITEM

"I've been using the workbooks for a few years now. They've allowed me to achieve some really crazy goals I've set for myself. They are a must-have if you want to create an amazing year."

— **Denise Duffield-Thomas, author of** *"Lucky Bitch"*

A GUIDE TO BUILD MY BUSINESS

"Leonie Dawson's workbooks are SO powerful. I have used them every year for the last 8 years. I gush about them all the time. Whatever I put in these workbooks ends up becoming destiny. I cannot recommend them enough"

-Hibiscus Moon, author + crystal expert

HIGHLY RECOMMENDED

"I love these workbooks and have used them for years for my life and business. Whatever I write in there ends up happening. I highly recommend them."

— **Nathalie Lussier, entrepreneur, AccessAlly**

TRULY TOOK MY BUSINESS TO THE NEXT LEVEL!

"[This] workbook was the swift kick in the butt I needed to start looking at my business for what it really is— a huge source of joy in my life. Since doing the workbook I have tripled my monthly income and found financial freedom in my business!"

- Flora Sage, author, speaker + coach

HELPED ME CREATE AN AUTHENTIC BUSINESS!

"[This] workbook helped me identify what really mattered to me in my business and life, and helped me develop a business that was completely grounded in those values."

- Katie Cowan, Symphony Law's founder

I CANNOT TELL YOU THE IMPACT THAT THE WORKBOOK HAD ON MY BUSINESS!

"Leonie's straight talking, comprehensible approach to business made it easy for me to take all the steps I had either been avoiding or wasn't even aware I should be taking. Within a month I had not only been brave enough to set income targets for the first time, I had met and overshot them!"

- Kate Beddow, holistic therapist

EASY & POWERFUL WAY TO TRANSFORM!

"Thanks to Leonie's intuitive and business skills I have grown both in my business and in my personal life. I feel so much more in tune with my needs and I've gained so much clarity. It is so clear to me now that anything is possible. Let the magic begin!"

- Karina Ladet, intuitive healer

AMAZED AT THE IMPACT IT HAD! "Wow! I'm a big forward thinker and straight away this shifted my thinking because first up I had to reflect on the year just past which was incredibly powerful. . . I ended up purchasing copies for several of my coaching clients so they could enjoy the experience of completing their own workbook too!"

- Belinda Jackson, business strategist

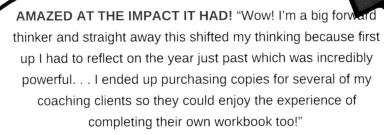

I WAS BLOWN AWAY!

"To be honest, I was a bit skeptical when I bought the workbook. However, I was BLOWN AWAY by the value offered. After going through the workbooks, I had a clear plan for achieving both my personal and business goals. I'm now calmer, more focused, and more productive. My monthly income has more than doubled!"

- Shay de Silva, fitness coach + founder of Fast Fitness To Go

The New Year stands Before us, Like A chapter in A BOOK waiting to Be Written. we can help WRITE THAT STORY by setting goals.

— Melody Beattie

CONGRATULATIONS

ON choosing this book. On stepping up to make your **dreams** come true! On saying **YES!** to being a <u>CONSCIOUS</u> <u>CREATOR</u> of your own Life + Business.

BUSINESS does not have to **BREAK** you, your finances, your work/Life Balance or your spirit. Instead business can be enormously **joyful**, **$ Profitable** + a ➡ force for **good** in the WORLD.

❓ What do you need to do to make that shift happen?

Step 1: Take the Vow ?

I, _____
                NAME
do solemnly swear that I am committed to my own success. That I am 100% Responsible for my actions + subsequent results. By aligning my actions with my intentions, I become a Powerful Creator of My Own Destiny.

_____   _____
      SIGNED   DATE

②. Fill out this workbook

It is NOT ENOUGH to just BUY it & use it as a paper-weight.

You must **actually** **DO THE THING** & **FILL IT OUT!**

③. Set a Deadline

JAN
30

Decide **NOW** when you will have this workbook Completed by

I commit to finishing this workbook by:

_____
DATE

_____
SIGNED

④ Schedule in Your Goals

Once you've set goals:

Take a look at YouR YEARLY calendaR. Map out some of when YouR Big goals could happen.

Look at YOUR daily + weekly schedule to Build in Goal Getting time!

⑤ Surround YOURSELF with other GOAL-GETTERS

gift this Book TO FRIENDS!

StaRt A woRKBook GROUP!

join MY woRKBook Facebook group!

"YOU aRe the AVERage OF the 5 PeoPle You SPeND YOUR time with. Make them gOOD ONES!"
-JIM ROHN

6. REGULARLY LOOK AT YOUR GOALS!

The MORE YOU REMEMBER & REVIEW YOUR GOALS, the faster they will come true! It will help You align YOUR DAILY habits in the direction of YOUR DREAMS.

CARRY THIS BOOK WITH YOU UNTIL it is DOG-eared & Well LOVED ♥

CREATE A Desktop wallpaper that reminds You of Your goals

KEEP A NOTE ON YOU with YOUR TOP 3 GOALS YOU are WORKING ON ★

USE the MONTHLY CHECK-iN WORKsheets in this Book!

A **Millionaire** LOOKS AT THEIR GOALS **ONCE** A DAY.

A **Billionaire** LOOKS AT THEIR GOALS **TWICE** A DAY.

Want to BE in the top (1%) of achievers?

80% of PEOPLE DON'T EVEN THINK of GOALS

16% THINK OF GOALS BUT DON'T write them down

3% write down their goals but never look at them again

JUST 1% WRITE DOWN their goals AND REGULARLY REVIEW THEM. THESE PEOPLE ARE AMONG THE ★ highest ★ Achievers

Why LEARN from LEONIE?

- ♥ Internationally best-selling author
- ♥ Has created over $14 Million in Revenue in 10 hours a week
- ♥ Winner of AusMumpreneur's Businesses Making A Difference Award Global Brand Award & People's Choice Business Coach Award
- ♥ Creator of the Brilliant Biz + Life academy *

DO YOU NEED to fill out this whole book for it to work?

YES  NO

Something is better than NOTHING!
Do what you can or are called to.
The MORE you put in, the MORE You will
get out of it. ♥ YOUR FUTURE
SELF will thank you ♥

ReSults YOU CAN get FROM USING the WORKBOOKS

Increased income

Increased AudieNce

Reach your Biz goals faster

Better WORK/LIFE Balance

Increased Self ConfiDeNce

MORe clarity

Renewed PASSiON

INSeRT YOUR deaRest wish here

Have YOUR Best year yet in Biz!

- - - - - - - - - - -

Let's Review the PAST YEAR

WHY REVIEW
the Past Year?

So often we want to →JUMP straight into setting NEW goals, dreaming NEW DREAMS before we do the

ALL IMPORTANT WORK

of reviewing the past year.

To leap FORWARD into the future, we must first:

1. KNOW where we are Right Now

2. Take the time to mine for clarity insights Lessons from the Past Year. It is a veritable treasure chest of GOLDEN WISDOM just waiting for You!

Let's PLAY
EVERYBODY'S
faVouRite
game Show

↓

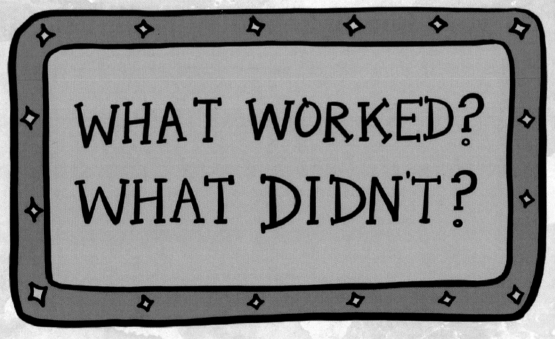

WHAT WORKED?
WHAT DIDN'T?

WHAT WORKED?

WHAT DIDN'T?

PRODUCTION
MAKING OR SOURCING YOUR PRODUCT OR SERVICE

STAFF
EMPLOYEES + CONTRACTORS

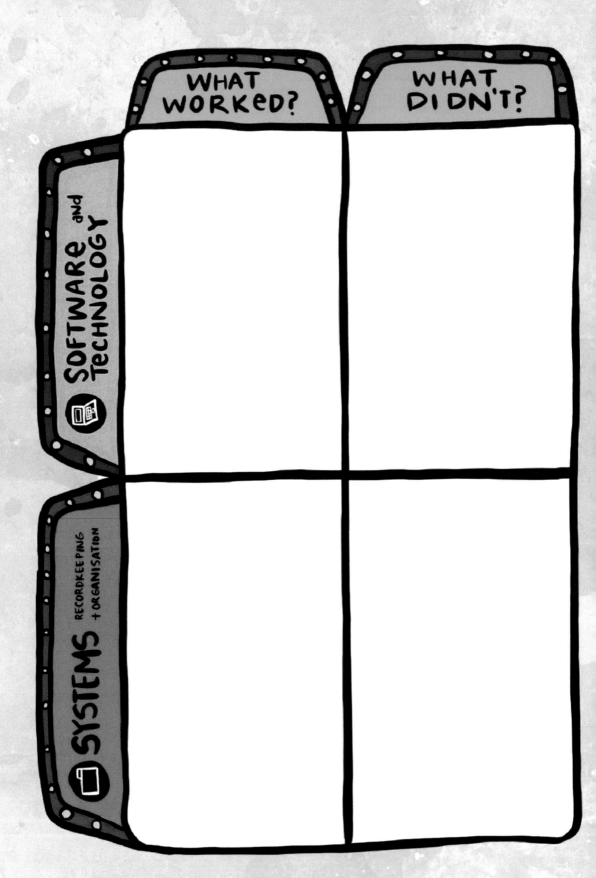

WHAT WORKED?

WHAT DIDN'T?

SOFTWARE and TECHNOLOGY

SYSTEMS
RECORDKEEPING + ORGANISATION

	WHAT WORKED?	WHAT DIDN'T?
DAILY WORK ROUTINE		
OFFICE SPACE		

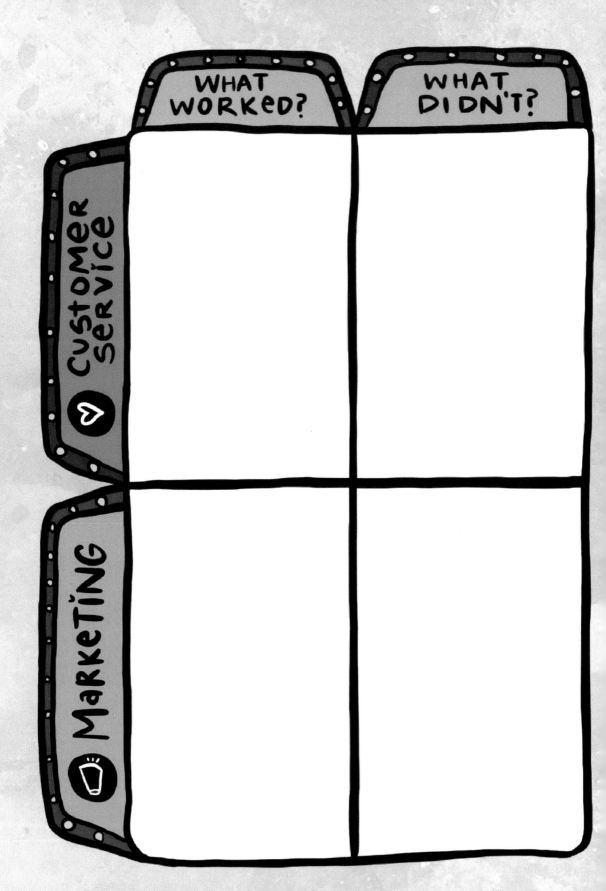

WHAT WORKED?

WHAT DIDN'T?

CUSTOMER SERVICE

MARKETING

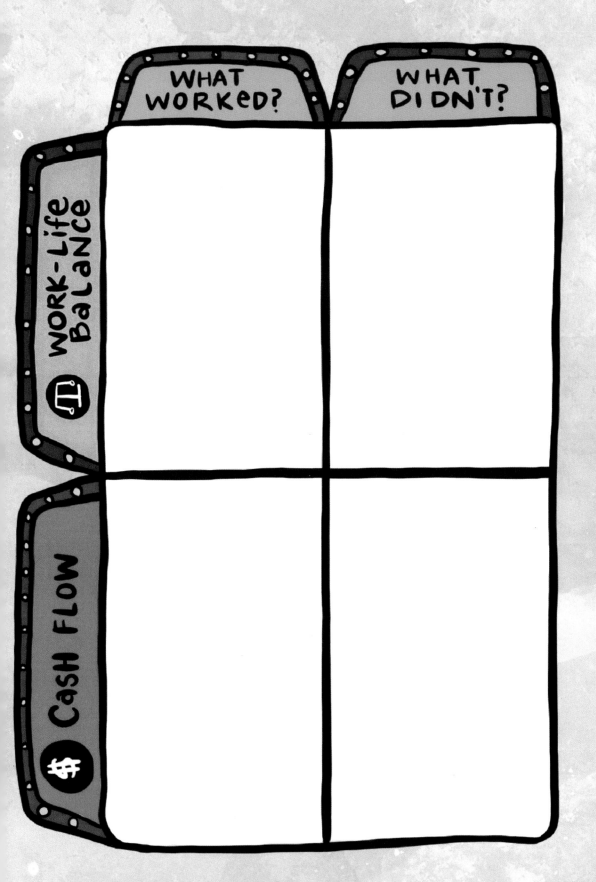

WHAT WORKED?

WHAT DIDN'T?

WORK-LIFE BALANCE

CASH FLOW

DEEP BREATH...

OK love... are you **READY?** It's time for us to **LOOK** at our 💰 **MONEY!** ♡

Now, before your chest constricts & your heart races & your fingers want to flick through this section... ↘

PLEASE KNOW YOU ABSOLUTELY CAN do THIS!

① You ARE NOT ALONE in feeling LIKE THIS!

Most people prefer to ignore their finances & want to stick their heads in the sand

② Looking at OUR NUMBERS is exactly what's needed to:
☑ increase income
☑ decrease expenses
☑ grow profit.

So powerful!

Finances

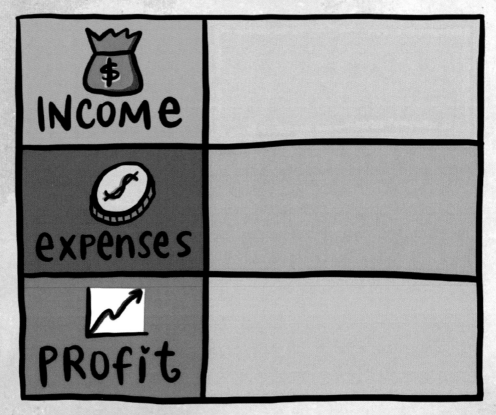 INCOME	
expenses	
PROFIT	

Create a pie chart of your expenses & profit levels

income flow

What did you earn each month?

JAN: _____
FEB: _____
MAR: _____
APR: _____
MAY: _____
June: _____

JULY: _____
Aug: _____
Sept: _____
Oct: _____
Nov: _____
Dec: _____

Sketch a line graph to see the FLOW!

$

JAN FEB MARCH APR MAY JUN JUL AUG SEP OCT NOV DEC

29

WHAT WERE YOUR BEST-SELLING PRODUCTS/SERVICES LAST YEAR?

OFFERING NAME	HOW MUCH IT MADE
1.	
2.	
3.	
4.	
5.	

Create a **Pie Chart** of how your top offerings sold

HOW MUCH DID YOUR audience grow in the last year?

Platform	Current #	HOW MUCH DID it GROW?
Mailing List		
FaceBook		

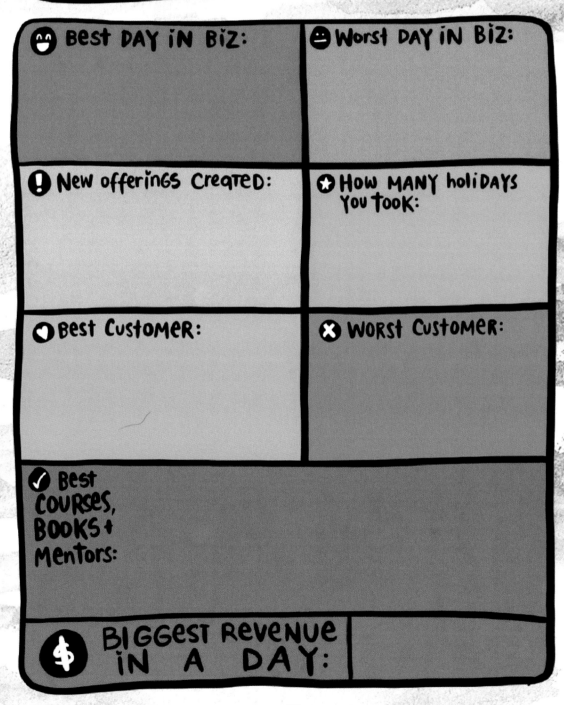

Let's REVIEW the last year! ✓

😃 BEST DAY IN BIZ:

😐 Worst DAY IN BIZ:

❗ New offerings CreateD:

⭐ HOW MANY holiDAYS You took:

🤍 Best Customer:

❌ WORST Customer:

✔ Best COURSES, BOOKS + Mentors:

💲 BIGGEST Revenue IN A DAY:

★ UNPLANNED SUCCESSES:

❗ BiggestT MiSTAKES:

⬆ What do you want to do MORE of?

⬇ What do you want to do LESS of?

◑ What helped most with STRESS?

♡ How did your biz support diversity + inclusion?

◐ How did your biz REDUCE its environmental impACt?

☾ How MUCH did your biz donate to charity?

 What are YOUR **BIZ ACCOMPLISHMENTS** from the past year?

What was the WORST THING about your biz in the last year?

what did YOU LEARN FROM it?

What was the BEST THING about your biz in the past year?

what did YOU LEARN FROM it? YOU LEARN

what AREAS of YOUR BIZ felt OUT of WHACK OR CRAZY-MAKING over the last YEAR?

what could BE OR fix DONE to change these AREAS?

What Do You NEED to WRITE, JOURNAL OR RANT about to feel clEAR About YOUR BiZ from the last YEAR?

A PAGE for Gratitude

DRAW, WRITE, illustrate OR ADD photos of EVERYTHING You are grateful for IN Your BIZ from the past year...

COMPLETION CIRCLE

Place your hand in the circle.

invoking the year AHEAD

It's time to DREAM a NEW DREAM. It's time to create a BRILLIANT, Shining YEAR for YOU + YOUR WORLD. First comes the THOUGHT, then comes the WORD, then the ACTION. ARE YOU READY? ☐ YES ☐ NO

MY finance GOALS

Finances

It's time to cast your mind forward & consider how you want your business finances to look in the next year. You don't have to guess it perfectly. just give yourself something to AIM for. The following pages will help you brainstorm these numbers in more detail. Let's PLAY + VISION in numbers!

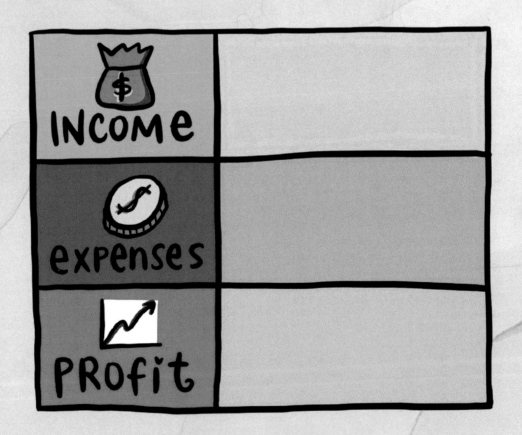

INCOME	
expenses	
PROFIT	

EXPENSES budgeting

It's time to do some estimates of your biz costs.
It's OK if these change over time!

Biz expense	estimate
Your Salary	
Staff	
Rent	
Software	
Web Hosting	
Advertising	

finance health check-up

Do You have A BOOKKEEPER & ACCOUNTANT?   ☐ ☐

Do You NEED to UPGRADE YouR Accountant?   ☐ ☐

ARE You eliGiBLE foR any Government GRants?   ☐ ☐

Do You NEED CREDit CARDS OR LOANS foR YouR BIZ To HELP WITH CASHFLOW AS You GRow?   ☐ ☐

Do You Set WEEKLY, Monthly & YeaRly Money GOALS? (PRO TIP: USe THE Monthly CHECK-IN WORKSHEETS at the eND of this BOOK!)   ☐ ☐

Is it time to Move to CLOUD-BASED ACCOUNTiNG SoftWARE OR INVOICING?   ☐ ☐

Do You NEED to CONSIDER A Better BuSiNESS/ COMPANY/tRuSt Set UP?   ☐ ☐

Do You NEED to iNCREASE YOUR PRICES?   ☐ ☐

Do You NEED to iMProve YouR DEBT COLLECTION?   ☐ ☐

Do You NEED to INVOICE MORE REGULARLY?   ☐ ☐

Do You NEED to iMProve YOUR BUSINESS FINANCES & CASHFLOW eDUCATION?   ☐ ☐

Do You NEED to Review WHICH OF YouR PRODUCTS/SeRVICES ARE MOST PROFITABLE?   ☐ ☐

iNCOME Possibilities

Play around with different products, sales numbers & prices to see what feels like the right fit for you to hit your revenue goal!

OFFERING	Price	#Sold	TOTAL
i.e. Artwork prints	$60	100	$6,000
GRAND Total			

What's the most CHALLENGING part of BIZ finances CURRENTLY?

What could be done to SOLVE it?

How MUCH DO YOU CURRENTLY HAVE IN BUSINESS SAVINGS?

How MUCH DO YOU WANT IN BUSINESS SAVINGS BY THE END OF THE YEAR?

What INCOME STREAMS do You Want to CREATE IN YOUR BIZ this YEAR?

Calculate YOUR COMPANY'S NET WORTH

Oh how fun! Let's look at the current net worth of YOUR business. ReMemBer to do this Just FOR YOUR Business, & do one for your life as well in the Life Goals WORKBOOK. And REMEMBER Your company's net worth is not YOUR Souls worth - You are infinitely precious!

ASSETS (what you own)	$ WORTH
Equipment	
Stock	
Cash	
Total Assets	$

LIABILITIES (what you owe)	$ COST
Credit Cards	
Loans	
Total Liabilities	$

NET WORTH (Assets Minus liabilities)	

the HANDY-DANDY TAX PLANNER

Sometimes the things we Don't Know can scare us... especially tax! As Soon as we Know what we aRe Dealing with though, it all becomes DOABLE & SolveABLE. WORK WITH YOUR ACCOUNTANT to get estimates on WHEN tax is Due & How MUCH it will be. THEN YOU CAN PLAN FOR it BETTER & have LESS CASHFLOW freakouts when tax is Due!

JaN	FeB	MaR
APR	MAY	JUNE
JUL	AUG	SeP
oct	NOV	Dec

(You Might like to ADD these to YOUR caleNDAR OR YEARLY WALL PLANNER too! ♥♥♥)

MAKE A LIST OF WAYS YOU COULD IMPROVE YOUR FINANCES BASED ON this CHAPTER...

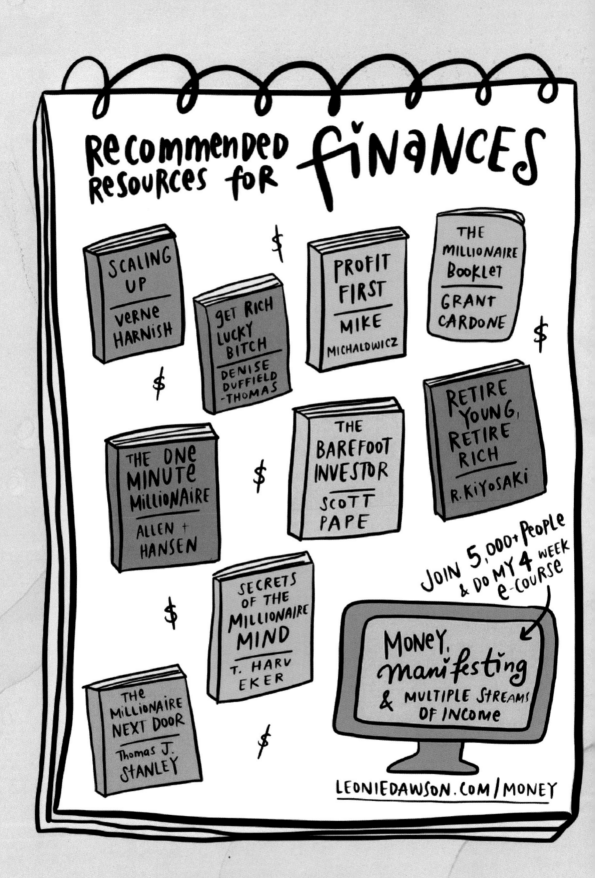

CReate a VISiON that Makes you want to JUMP out of Bed in the Morning!

MY TEAM & SUPPORT GOALS

Have you got the staff or contractors you need in your business now?

Yes ☐   No ☐

WHAT'S WORKING WELL WITH YOUR TEAM RIGHT NOW?	WHAT'S NOT WORKING? HOW CAN YOU IMPROVE IT?

WHAT ADDITIONAL SUPPORT do you need from your team?

Do you have ANY ROLES you need to fill this year?

Support Check-In

	Yes	No
DO YOU HAVE A MENTOR YOU CAN TURN TO?	☐	☐
HAVE YOU OUTGROWN YOUR MENTOR?	☐	☐
DO YOU HAVE A MASTERMIND OF PEOPLE YOU CAN BRAINSTORM WITH & RECEIVE ADVICE FROM?	☐	☐
IF YOU HAVE CHILDREN, DO YOU HAVE ENOUGH SUPPORT WITH CHILDCARE?	☐	☐
DO YOU HAVE AN ACCOUNTABILITY PARTNER?	☐	☐

What DO YOU NEED to **thrive** as a CEO over the Next YEAR?

WHO CAN YOU vent to when thinGs Get HARD?

What KIND of MENTOR DO YOU NEED?

BRAINSTORM WAYS YOU CAN CREATE OR FIND A MASTERMIND* OR MENTOR:

*A MASTERMIND IS A GROUP OF PEOPLE WHO MEET (ONLINE OR IN REAL LIFE) TO SUPPORT EACH OTHER'S BUSINESS OR PERSONAL GROWTH. CAN BE PAID OR FREE.

RECOMMENDED RESOURCES FOR
team & support

THRIVE — Arianna Huffington

SCALING UP — VERNE HARNISH

PEAK — CHIP CONLEY

TOP GRADING — Bradford Smart

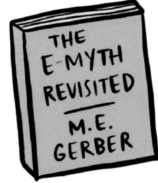

THE E-MYTH REVISITED — M.E. GERBER

DELIVERING HAPPINESS — TONY HSEIH

NO B.S. TIME MANAGEMENT FOR ENTREPRENEURS — D. KENNEDY

FOUR HOUR WORK WEEK — T. FERRISS

THE MILLION-DOLLAR ONE-PERSON BUSINESS — E. POFELDT

& MORE RESOURCES AT LEONIEDAWSON.COM

YOUR
glorious
life is
→ RIGHT HERE ←
READY to BE

chosen.

MY

Get Organised

GOALS

It's Time To Get ORGANiSED!

Use this checklist to Review where you NEED to get ORGANiSED in your business. Don't get OVERWHELMED if there's a lot to get SoRTeD... You can WORK on ONE piece at a time & by the end of the year, you will be even more ORGANiSED!

ACCOUNTiNG

	YES	NO
Do you have accounting software that works for you?	○	○
Can you easily access statistics on how much income, expenses & taxes your biz is generating?	○	○
Do you know when taxes are due?	○	○
Do you pay taxes late?	○	○
Do you have an accountant & bookkeeper?	○	○
Do you have a place to store both physical & digital invoices & receipts?	○	○
Is your business ready for an audit?	○	○
Do you have recurring tasks in your calendar for when taxes + bookkeeping are due?	○	○

GENERAL

	YES	NO
Does Your Business have Standard Operating Procedures (how-to instructions) on all Your Biz tasks?	◯	◯
Do You have A physical & digital filing System so You can easily find documents, photos & files?	◯	◯
Do You REGULARLY Back Up Your most important Data (i.e. website or MAILING List)?	◯	◯
Do You have a system for organising, responding to & filing all incoming mail & email?	◯	◯

TECH

	YES	NO
Can You easily sell Your products using Your website?	◯	◯
Have You recently reviewed all of Your software subscriptions to see if You are paying for anything you No longer need?	◯	◯
Do You have a system for making sure Your computers, website & plugins are updated to the Latest version to prevent bugs + hackers?	◯	◯
Are You using cloud storage?	◯	◯
Are You Using a password storage app like LastPass or Dashlane?	◯	◯

LEGALITIES

	YES	NO
Do You have all the Business Registrations You need?	○	○
Do You have the insurances You need?	○	○
Do You need to change Your business, company or trust structure?	○	○
Do You need an exit strategy or succession plan?	○	○
Do You have a written plan on what needs to happen if You or Your business partner suffer from illness, accident or (GAWD FORBID!) death?	○	○

CUSTOMERS

	YES	NO
Do You have a DATABASE that records Your customers' contact details & Purchases?	○	○
Do You have a system to onboard, follow up & offboard customers?	○	○
Do You have a system to ensure all customer emails & phone calls are responded to promptly?	○	○
Do You have a system to regularly ask customers for referrals + reviews?	○	○
Do You have templated responses to answer Your customers' frequently asked questions?	○	○

MAKE A LIST OF WAYS YOU COULD GET ORGANISED BASED ON this CHAPTER...

MY
BOUNDARIES &
Work-Life Balance
GOALS

This YEAR  GIVE MYSELF PERMISSION IN MY BIZ to:

— PERMISSION SLIP —

HOLIDAY PLANNER

TAKING HOLIDAYS IS HUGELY IMPORTANT FOR YOUR MENTAL VIBRANCE, CREATIVITY & JOY FOR LIFE.

HOW MANY DAYS HOLIDAY WILL YOU TAKE THIS YEAR?

WHEN?

WHAT DO YOU NEED TO DO TO MAKE THEM HAPPEN?

what SELF CARE RULES WILL I have? ♥

NO WORKING at NIGHT

READ NON-BIZ BOOKS ON WEEKENDS! ♥

NO PHONE IN BEDROOM

Add YOUR OWN HERE

GO TO BED

eaRLY

I will only work ____ hours a week ♥

NO WORK ON

Adventure Saturdays | REST Sundays!
weekends

TIMES/DAYS that are WORK FREE:
_____
_____
_____
_____
_____
_____
_____

BUY & WEAR a badge like this ↘

GET a GLORIOUS LIFE ♥

I will LIMIT LIVE events + networking to ONLY:

____ A MONTH/YEAR

TIME REVIEW

Now is a GREAT time to REVIEW where you spend your time & how you'd like to spend it in the coming year.

Let's make PIE CHARTS to help you visualise!

HOW YOU currently SPEND YOUR Business HOURS

HOW YOU WiSH TO SPEND YOUR Business HOURS

What are YOU GOING to STOP doing this YEAR in YOUR business?

If YOU want to start creating NEW things, a NEW energy, expansion OR era in YOUR biz, YOU need to clear out the OLD.

You need to get RID of old:

HABITS   PROJECTS   OFFERINGS   BELIEFS

TASKS   SYSTEMS   METHODS

that aren't helping you move forward. Add what YOU will STOP doing BELOW...

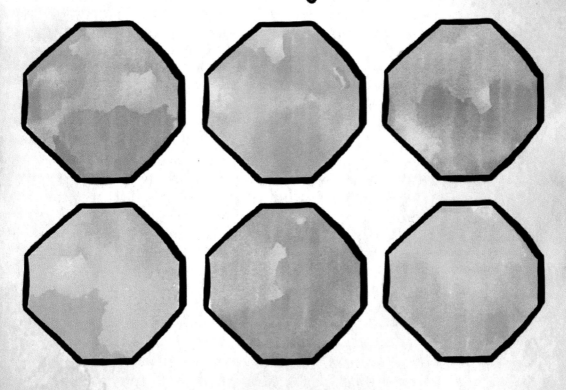

INSIDE YOU THERE
is the (🌱 Seed) of a
Great Tree,
FAR   LARGER
& (more)   MaGNIF
             -icent
than   You can
POS   SIBLY
👁   SEE
RIGHt   NOW.

MY GOAL Getter habits

WHAT joyful & NOURISHING HABITS WOULD YOU LIKE to cultivate over the next year? Don't worry about HOW HARD IT IS to FORM HABITS - what we'll be DOING instead is CREATING A POSTER to REMIND ourselves each DAY OF THE beautiful THINGS WE'D ♥ To DO!

SOME DAYS we might Do all of them, MOST DAYS we'll ONLY Get To some... OTHER DAYS we MAY Not Get to ANY.

all of this is gorgeous & fine ♥

It's Not ABOUT PERFECTION OR fAILURE. It's ABOUT REMINDING ourselves OF the toolkit of POSSIBILITIES available to us.

TIPS FOR CHOOSING HABITS

MAKE theM SOUND FUN! use WORDS that excite You!

MAKE YOUR HABITS Feel ACHIevaBLe! If it feels OVERWHELMING, KEEP it SIMPLER + MoRe DoABLE.

TRACK YOUR habits DAILY to STAY MOTIVATED.

CHOOSE HABITS that help You ACHIeve YOUR BIG GOALS.

71

ideas for goal getter HABiTS

write 750 words a DAY   Practise MiNDfULNESS

Exercise   GREEN SMOOThie   SiNGLe TASK

PROCESS emails ONCe A DAY   Declutter foR 10 MiNS

Eat fRESh fRUit & VegeS   Get iNbox to ZeRo

Stick to a 5 Sentence LiMit oN eMaiLS

WORK while DiSCONNeCted   JOURNaL dAiLY

Make a Piece of ART   Declutter YouR desk

FOLLOW a MORNiNG RoutiNe   Go foR A WALK

ReaD a chAPteR of A BooK   gratitUDe JoURNaL

HUG A PeRSoN oR a Pet   WRite A thank You NoTe

Connect with A FRIeND   DRiNk 8 GLaSSeS of WATER

WRite A DAiLY to Do List & iDeNtifY YOUR 3
M.I.T.s (MOST iMPORtANt tASKS)

Keep A tech-fRee BeDRooM   PRACtise A HobbY

PRACTiSe SeLf CaRe   COMPLiMeNt SomeONe

PERfORM a RaNDoM ACt OF KiNDNESS

MY goal getter HABITS

MY
EDUCATION
GOALS

WHAT DO YOU NEED to LEARN about this YEAR to PROPEL YOU & YOUR BUSINESS FORWARD?

WHAT COURSES, MASTERMIND OR COACHING DO YOU NEED to invest IN?

What BOOKS do You Want to READ this YEAR?

HOW MUCH **time** DO YOU NEED to Set ASiDe foR LEARNING?

WHAT DO YOU NEED TO DO to CReate & SupPoRt A BUSINESS that eaRNS YOUR INCOME GOAL?

RECOMMENDED RESOURCES FOR
education

Scaling Up
— VERNE HARNISH

GOOD TO GREAT
— J. Collins

Chill -PRENEUR
— DENISE DUFFIELD -THOMAS

BETTER THAN BEFORE
— G. RUBIN

SHARK TALES
— Barbara Corcoran

WORK LESS, MAKE MORE
— J. SCHRAMKO

FOUR HOUR WORK WEEK
— T. FERRISS

MY onLine courses

- MONEY, MANIFESTING & MULTIPLE STREAMS OF INCOME
- 40 DAYS TO CREATE & SELL YOUR E-COURSE
- 40 DAYS TO A FINISHED BOOK

LEONIEDAWSON.COM

TO MAKE YOUR
dreams
COME TRUE,
ALIGN YOUR
ACTIONS
WITH YOUR
INTENTIONS.

MY CUSTOMER GOALS

HOW COULD YOU IMPROVE YOUR CUSTOMER SERVICE this YEAR?

Where do Your CUSTOMERS Get "stuck" the Most? What do they COMPLAIN ABout? What could You Do to fix those PROBLEMS Before they happen?

How CAN You REWARD YOUR Most loYal Customers?

How CAN You CAPTURE & SHARE more of YouR
Customers' testiMONiALS & SUCCESS StoRies?

CUSTOMER LOVE DAY

Here at Leonie Dawson International, we love celebrating our clients with Customer Love Day!

It's a gorgeous ritual when we do extra special things to treat our customers.

Small things can make such a BIG difference in celebrating the people that make your business thrive.

IDEAS FOR SHOWING Customer Love

- ♥ Hold a PARTY
- ♥ Send out postcards
- ♥ Run a FREE workshop
- ♥ Send gifts to your most loyal customers
- ♥ Have a client-only SALE
- ♥ Make thank you phone calls

How will you show your customers ♥ love?

How often do you want to run it?

☐ Monthly ☐ Quarterly
☐ Bi-annual ☐ Annually

What date will it be?

(Then pop it in your calendar!)

👁 make
my own
dreams
come true.

MY MARKETING GOALS

HOW MUCH DO YOU
want your audience to grow this year?

Platform	Current #	HOW BIG DO YOU WANT IT TO BE?
Mailing List		
FaceBook		

What **AWARDS** do you want to apply for?

How MANY **ZINES** OR **NEWSLETTERS** will you send this YEAR?

What **FREE LEAD MAGNETS** will you CREATE this YEAR?

What OTHER **Marketing** goals do you HAVE for this YEAR?

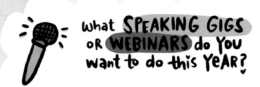 What **SPEAKING GIGS** OR **WEBINARS** do you want to do this YEAR?

 WHERE WOULD YOU LIKE **MEDIA MENTIONS** this YEAR?

 What **NETWORKING EVENTS** do you want to Attend this YEAR?

 NEW! What NEW PRODUCTS/SERVICES will you CREATE?

RECOMMENDED RESOURCES FOR
Marketing

DOT COM SECRETS
— RUSSELL BRUNSON

CA$H -vertising
— DREW ERIC WHITMAN

THE PSYCHOLOGY OF SELLING
— BRIAN TRACY

SHOW YOUR WORK!
— AUSTIN KLEON

INFLUENCE
— Robert Cialdini

THE ULTIMATE SALES LETTER
— D. Kennedy

THE ENTREPRENEUR'S GUIDE TO GETTING YOUR SHIT TOGETHER
— J. CARLTON

Join 5,000+ biz owners in my SALES STAR PROGRAM

LEONIEDAWSON.COM/SELL

Businesses

are RUN on a MOTOR of

COURAGE,

faith &

Determination.

MY
Do BetteR
GOALS

HOW MUCH **MONEY** DO YOU WANT YOUR BUSINESS TO DONATE THIS YEAR?

TO WHAT **CAUSES** DO YOU want to DONATE to?

DO YOU want to **DONATE** YOUR **SERVICES** OR **time** this YEAR? AND to WHERE?

_____

_____

_____

_____

WHAT WAYS CAN YOUR BUSINESS REDUCE ITS **ENVIRONMENTAL IMPACT** this YEAR?

Change The World
RECOMMENDED READING!

WILDING — isabella TREE

CREATING ROOM TO READ — J. WOODS

THIS IS NOT A DRILL EXTINCTION REBELLION

CHAPTER ONE — Daniel FLYNN

DARE TO LEAD — B. Brown

EVERY WOMAN'S GUIDE TO SAVING THE PLANET — NATALIE ISAACS

THE YEAR OF LESS — CAIT FLANDERS

BEYOND THE GENDER BINARY — A. VAID-MENON

EL DEAFO — CECE BELL

GENDER QUEER — MAIA KOBABE

QUEER — M.J. Barker & J. Scheele

QUICK + EASY GUIDE TO THEY/THEM PRONOUNS — A. BONJIOVANNI T. JIMERSON

QUICK + EASY GUIDE TO QUEER + TRANS IDENTITIES — MADY G. J.R. Zuckerberg

MORE gender, SEXUALITY, DISABILITY & TRANS READING at LEONIEDAWSON.COM/GENDER

Anti- RACIST
RECOMMENDED READING!

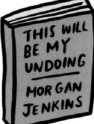

FOR MORE anti-Racist EDUCATION RESOURCES
GO TO www.LEONIEDAWSON.COM/RACISM

This world can change & (we) are the ones who will change it.

Rounding it all UP!

MY goals that are so **BIG + DARING** that im not even sure they are **POSSIBLE** are...

what are the **TOP 10** things you want to **DO** in the life of YOUR BIZ?

①

②

③

④

⑤

⑥

⑦

⑧

⑨

⑩

100 things to do!

These can be BIG goals or tiny ones...
a culmination of all your goals from this
workbook, or totally new ones. Just have
FUN & encourage yourself to stretch!

1. _____ ☐
2. _____ ☐
3 _____ ☐
[4.] _____ ☐
5 _____ ☐
6. _____ ☐
7. _____ ☐
8 _____ ☐
9 _____ ☐
10. _____ ☐
11 _____ ☐
12 _____ ☐
13 _____ ☐
14. _____ ☐

15. _____ ☐
16 _____ ☐
17. _____ ☐
18. _____ ☐
19. _____ ☐
20. _____ ☐
[21] _____ ☐
22. _____ ☐
23 _____ ☐
24. _____ ☐
25. _____ ☐
26. _____ ☐
27. _____ ☐
28 _____ ☐

29. _____

30. _____

31. _____

32. _____

33. _____

34. _____

35. _____

36. _____

37. _____

38. _____

39. _____

40. _____

41. _____

42. _____

43. _____

44. _____

45. _____

46. _____

47. _____

48. _____

49. _____

50. _____

51. _____

52. _____

53. _____

54. _____

55. _____

56. _____

57. _____

58. _____

59. _____

60. _____

61. _____

62. _____

63. _____

64. _____

65. _____

66. _____

67. _____

68. _____

69. _____ ☐
70. _____ ☐
71. _____ ☐
72. _____ ☐
73. _____ ☐
74. _____ ☐
75. _____ ☐
76. _____ ☐
77. _____ ☐
78. _____ ☐
79. _____ ☐
80. _____ ☐
81. _____ ☐
82. _____ ☐
83. _____ ☐
84. _____ ☐
85. _____ ☐
86. _____ ☐
87. _____ ☐
88. _____ ☐

89. _____ ☐
90. _____ ☐
91. _____ ☐
92. _____ ☐
93. _____ ☐
94. _____ ☐
95. _____ ☐
96. _____ ☐
97. _____ ☐
98. _____ ☐
99. _____ ☐
100. _____ ☐

Dream Big!

DReaM DaY

I wish this was an Assignment we were Given in school.
I wish we'd been taught to DREAM BIG & create the Life we want.
At least we are doing it Now. It's TIME.
I want You to write IN AS MUCH Detail AS possible
what YOUR DREAM DAY would look like. Where would
you Be? Who would you be with? How would you spend
your time? What would be YOUR DREAM WORK?
I promise you, this exercise is powerful. It's time to
Become AN EXPERT in you + YOUR DREAMS.

Annual Oracle Reading

I began giving myself yearly forecast readings in 2011. It amazed me how accurate + insightful it was as the year unfolded...

I've done it each year since with profound results... & I'd ♥ to invite you to TRY it out for yourself! ☆

♥ HOW TO DO YOUR OWN

1. Use whatever holy text or cards feel good to <u>your</u> heart

   Quran   Oracle cards   Poetry book   Sacred book

   Bible   TAROT   Affirmation deck

2. Connect to your personal source of divine guidance

3. Pull a card or open to a random page of book for each month

4. Write down the message for each month that feels most important ♥♥

JANUARY

FEBRUARY

MARCH

APRIL

may

june

july

august

September

October

November

December

DREAMBOARD

DreamBoards are an incredibly powerful tool for visualising what you wish to create. Not only can they be beautiful & inspiring to look at, but they will help you remember every single day your dreams & highest intentions. What you focus on becomes true!

SUPPLIES You will NEED ♥

A piece of cardboard, paper or canvas in the size that feels right to you

GLUE

SCISSORS

Magazines, Newspapers, photos + images

add a little blend of OPENNESS, ☆ courage, JOY + a sprinkle of hope. ♥

Search through MAGAZINES for images + WORDS of things, people, feelings & experiences you'd like to draw into your life for the next year ♥♥♥

Cut out the images that lift you up, inspire you + make you feel RADIANT ♥ Ignore everything that feels like a SHOULD!

ARRANGE on your board until it feels JUST RIGHT to your spirit then GLUE! glue

PLACE it WHERE you can see it DAILY. On your DESK, BY your BED - even on the back of your toilet Door!

You can also use the following page as a DREAMBOARD to keep with your WORKBOOK

EACH DAY, take ACTIONS that bring YOU CLOSER to your DREAMS

WATCH as your dreams MAGICALLY APPEAR!

You can also use PINTEREST as an online dream BOARD - OR make a digital collage using Canva!

MY MINI PORTABLE DREAMBOARD

What To Do When EVERYTHING SUCKS

There's going to be hard moments in the year ahead. We can prep for them by brainstorming what helps us shift our mood. Our feelings can change in a moment. Fickle things they are - generated by our environment, body, situation & perspective. Let's brainstorm what gentle changes can help you shift the mood when everything sucks!

LEONIE'S LIST OF DESUCKIFICATION
- ♥ Go outside
- ♥ Smell lavender
- ♥ Eat something green 🌱
- ♥ Have a shower
- ♥ Do 10 mins of stretching

CUT OUT + PUT IN A HANDY PLACE (YOUR PURSE OR PHONE) FOR A SUCKTASTIC EMERGENCY

THINGS TO DO when THE SUCKIES STRIKE

How

to make those

beautiful

goals

of YOURS

come

true!

How To Make Your Goals Happen!

Setting your Goal is just the FIRST step in birthing your dreams into the world.

As you get started in making your goals happen you may experience feelings like:

Overwhelm   Confusion   Paralysis   FREAK OUT

This can happen when we see OUR GOAL as just ONE TASK on our to do list.

To Do
☐ write book

In REALITY a BIG GOAL like this has MANY indidual tasks to COMPLETE. It looks more like:

TO DO
☐ Brainstorm book chapters
☐ Gather references
☐ Decide on word processor
☐ Set daily writing goal
☐ write 1,000 words...

You can't eat a **BURGER** in one bite.

You can't **CLIMB A MOUNTAIN** in one step.

Goals, mountains + burgers are all the same. They are accomplished one step, one bite, one task at a time.

WHEN IN DOUBT OR PARALYSIS, BREAK THE TASKS DOWN INTO EVEN SMALLER TASKS THAT TAKE LESS THAN 10 MIN TO DO!

<u>TO DO</u>
- ☐ Create a new document
- ☐ Write 3 bullet points

MAKING MICRO TASKS LIKE THIS can sometimes really help spur me into Action! I ♥ ticking things off ☑

Magic Momentum Map

Write Goal Here ↳

 I'd like to have it Completed BY:

_____

What DAILY HABITS will help me get there?

Circle What Would Help You:

Co-work Space

Say NO to More things

Social MEDIA Sabbatical

Accountability Partner

COACH

RETREAT

Go PUBLIC WITH YOUR GOAL

 How will you CELEBRATE when you get there?

Project Tracker

COLOUR YOUR PROGRESS AS YOU GO! ♥

10%. 20%. 30%. 40%. 50%. 60%. 70%. 80%. 90%.

FINISH!

BREAK YOUR GOAL INTO MICROTASKS! ♡

ADD DEADLINES FOR MICROTASKS!

HIGHLIGHT the most URGENT TASKS

☆ Magic Momentum Map

Write Goal Here ↳

I'd like to have it completed BY:

_____

What DAILY HABITS will help me get there?

Circle What Would Help You:

Co-work Space

Say No to More things

Social MEDIA Sabbatical

Accountability Partner

COACH

RETREAT

Go PUBLIC WITH YOUR GOAL

How will you CELEBRATE when YOU GET THERE?

Project Tracker

COLOUR YOUR PROGRESS as YOU GO! ♥

10% 20% 30% 40% 50% 60% 70% 80% 90% FINISH!

BREAK YOUR GOAL INTO MICROTASKS!

- [ ] _____
- [ ] _____
- [ ] _____
- [ ] _____
- [ ] _____
- [ ] _____
- [ ] _____
- [ ] _____
- [ ] _____
- [ ] _____
- [ ] _____
- [ ] _____
- [ ] _____
- [ ] _____
- [ ] _____
- [ ] _____
- [ ] _____
- [ ] _____
- [ ] _____
- [ ] _____
- [ ] _____
- [ ] _____
- [ ] _____

- [ ] _____
- [ ] _____
- [ ] _____
- [ ] _____
- [ ] _____
- [ ] _____
- [ ] _____
- [ ] _____
- [ ] _____
- [ ] _____
- [ ] _____
- [ ] _____
- [ ] _____
- [ ] _____
- [ ] _____
- [ ] _____
- [ ] _____
- [ ] _____
- [ ] _____
- [ ] _____
- [ ] _____
- [ ] _____

ADD DEADLINES FOR MICROTASKS!

HIGHLIGHT the most URGENT TASKS

☆ Magic Momentum Map

write Goal Here ↳

I'd like to have it COMPLETED BY:

What DAILY HABITS will help me get there?

Circle What Would Help You:

Co-work Space

Say No to More things

Social MEDIA Sabbatical

Accountability Partner

COACH

RETREAT

Go PUBLIC WITH YOUR GOAL

How will you CELEBRATE when you get there?

Project Tracker

COLOUR YOUR PROGRESS as YOU GO! ♥

10%. 20%. 30%. 40%. 50%. 60%. 70%. 80%. 90%.

FINISH!

BREAK YOUR GOAL iNTO MiCROTASKS!

- ☐ _____
- ☐ _____
- ☐ _____
- ☐ _____
- ☐ _____
- ☐ _____
- ☐ _____
- ☐ _____
- ☐ _____
- ☐ _____
- ☐ _____
- ☐ _____
- ☐ _____
- ☐ _____
- ☐ _____
- ☐ _____
- ☐ _____
- ☐ _____
- ☐ _____
- ☐ _____
- ☐ _____
- ☐ _____

- ☐ _____
- ☐ _____
- ☐ _____
- ☐ _____
- ☐ _____
- ☐ _____
- ☐ _____
- ☐ _____
- ☐ _____
- ☐ _____
- ☐ _____
- ☐ _____
- ☐ _____
- ☐ _____
- ☐ _____
- ☐ _____
- ☐ _____
- ☐ _____
- ☐ _____
- ☐ _____
- ☐ _____
- ☐ _____

ADD DeaDLiNes for MiCROTaSKS!

HIGHLIGHT the most URGeNT TaSKS

A goal without a plan is just a wish.

👁 <u>DON'T</u> FOCUS ON WHAT I'M UP against.

👁 FOCUS ON MY GOALS + 👁 try to ignore tHE rest.

— VENUS WILLIAMS

Monthly Checkins

Remember this tasty tidbit from the start of this book?

It's (not enough) to just fill out this WORKBOOK & never look at it again.

80% of people don't even think of goals

16% don't write down their goals

3% write down their goals

1% write goals down + regularly review. These are among the Highest Achievers!

REMEMBER:

It's the 1% of the population who write down their goals AND regularly review them who are AMONG the → HIGHEST ACHIEVERS ←

And YOU are GOING to BE one of them. PULL OUT YOUR CALENDAR NOW + SET A RECURRING date IN YOUR calendar at the start of every MONTH. Come back here, fill out the WORKSHEET & have a monthly date with YOUR dreams ♥♥♥

The MONTHLY CHECK in sheets will keep YOU on tRACK, motivated + PRODUCTIVE. And YOu'll join that incredible 1% of people who know how to MAKE their dREAMS COME tRUE!

JANUARY BUSINESS
GOALS PLAN

INCOME GOAL for this MONTH:

Brainstorm how you could create it:

PRODUCT	PRICE	# SOLD	TOTAL

What DAILY HABITS would help?

HOW WILL YOU CELEBRATE WHEN YOU GET THERE?

WHAT DO YOU NEED TO DO TO GET THERE?

IT'S TIME TO REVIEW
January!

☆ What goals did you achieve in Jan?	☑ What goals do you want to have in FEB?

❓ What do you need to do to make them happen?	💗 What self care do you wish to feel in FEB?

FEBRUARY BUSINESS
GOALS PLAN

INCOME GOAL for this MONTH:

Brainstorm how you could create it:

PRODUCT	PRICE	# SOLD	TOTAL

What DAILY HABITS would help?

HOW WILL YOU CELEBRATE WHEN YOU GET tHERE?

WHAT DO YOU NEED TO DO TO GET tHERE?

- [ ]
- [ ]
- [ ]
- [ ]
- [ ]
- [ ]
- [ ]

- [ ]
- [ ]
- [ ]
- [ ]
- [ ]
- [ ]
- [ ]
- [ ]
- [ ]

IT'S TIME TO REVIEW

February

⭐ What goals did you achieve in FeB?	☑ What goals do you want to have in March?

❓ What do you need to do to make them happen?	💕 What self care do you wish to feel in MARCH?

· March · BUSINESS PLAN

GOALS

INCOME Goal for this MONTH:

Brainstorm how you could create it:

PRODUCT	PRICE	# SOLD	TOTAL

what DAILY HABITS would help?

HOW WILL YOU CELEBRATE WHEN YOU GET tHERE?

WHAT DO YOU NEED TO DO TO GET tHERE?

- [ ] _____
- [ ] _____
- [ ] _____
- [ ] _____
- [ ] _____
- [ ] _____
- [ ] _____

- [ ] _____
- [ ] _____
- [ ] _____
- [ ] _____
- [ ] _____
- [ ] _____
- [ ] _____
- [ ] _____
- [ ] _____

IT'S TIME TO REVIEW

March

☆ **What goals did you achieve in March?**	☑ **What goals do you want to have in APRIL?**
❓ **What do you need to do to make them happen?**	🖤 **What self care do you wish to feel in April?**

APRIL BUSINESS PLAN

GOALS

INCOME GOAL for this MONTH:

Brainstorm how you could create it:

PRODUCT	PRICE	# SOLD	TOTAL

What DAILY HABITS would help?

HOW WILL YOU CELEBRATE WHEN YOU GET THERE?

WHAT DO YOU NEED TO DO TO GET THERE?

- [ ]
- [ ]
- [ ]
- [ ]
- [ ]
- [ ]

- [ ]
- [ ]
- [ ]
- [ ]
- [ ]
- [ ]
- [ ]
- [ ]
- [ ]

IT'S TIME TO REVIEW

APRIL

⭐ What goals did you achieve in APRIL?	☑ What goals do you want to have in MAY?

❓ What do you need to do to make them happen?	💙 What self care do you wish to feel in MAY?

May BUSINESS PLAN

GOALS

INCOME GOAL for this MONTH:

Brainstorm how you could create it:

PRODUCT	PRICE	# SOLD	TOTAL

what DAILY HABITS would help?

HOW WILL YOU CELEBRATE when YOU Get tHERE?

WHAT DO YOU NEED TO DO TO GET tHERE?

☐
☐
☐
☐
☐
☐
☐

☐
☐
☐
☐
☐
☐
☐
☐
☐

IT'S TIME TO REVIEW

MAY

☆ What goals did you achieve in May?	☑ What goals do you want to have in June?

❓ What do you need to do to make them happen?	💕 What self care do you wish to feel in June?

JUNE BUSINESS PLAN GOALS

INCOME Goal for this MONTH:

Brainstorm how you could create it:

PRODUCT	PRICE	# SOLD	TOTAL

what DAILY HABITS would help?

HOW WILL YOU CELEBRATE WHEN YOU GET tHERE?

WHAT DO YOU NEED TO DO TO GET tHERE?

- [ ]
- [ ]
- [ ]
- [ ]
- [ ]
- [ ]
- [ ]
- [ ]

- [ ]
- [ ]
- [ ]
- [ ]
- [ ]
- [ ]
- [ ]
- [ ]
- [ ]
- [ ]

IT'S TIME TO REVIEW
JUNE

⭐ What goals did you achieve in June?	☑ What goals do you want to have in JULY?

❓ What do you need to do to make them happen?	💕 What self care do you wish to feel in JULY?

JULY BUSINESS
GOALS PLAN

INCOME GOAL for this MONTH:

Brainstorm how you could create it:

PRODUCT	PRICE	# SOLD	TOTAL

what DAILY HABITS would help?

HOW WILL YOU CELEBRATE WHEN YOU GET tHERE?

WHAT DO YOU NEED TO DO TO GET tHERE?

- ☐
- ☐
- ☐
- ☐
- ☐
- ☐
- ☐
- ☐

- ☐
- ☐
- ☐
- ☐
- ☐
- ☐
- ☐
- ☐
- ☐

IT'S TIME TO REVIEW

★ JULY ★

☆ What goals did you achieve in July?	☑ What goals do you want to have in August?

❓ What do you need to do to make them happen?	💗 What self care do you wish to feel in August?

AUGUST BUSINESS
GOALS PLAN

INCOME GOAL for this MONTH:

Brainstorm how you could create it:

PRODUCT	PRICE	# SOLD	TOTAL

what DAILY HABITS would help?

HOW WILL YOU CELEBRATE WHEN YOU GET THERE?

WHAT DO YOU NEED TO DO TO GET THERE?

IT'S TIME TO REVIEW

AUGUST

☆ What goals did you achieve in August?

☑ What goals do you want to have in Sept?

❓ What do you need to do to make them happen?

💙 What self care do you wish to feel in Sept?

· September · BUSINESS

GOALS PLAN

INCOME Goal for this MONTH:

Brainstorm how you could create it:

PRODUCT	PRICE	# SOLD	TOTAL

what DAILY HABITS would help?

HOW WILL YOU CELEBRATE WHEN YOU GET THERE?

WHAT DO YOU NEED TO DO TO GET THERE?

IT'S TIME TO REVIEW

September

⭐ **What goals did you achieve in September?**

☑ **What goals do you want to have in Oct?**

❓ **What do you need to do to make them happen?**

💙 **What self care do you wish to feel in Oct?**

October BUSINESS GOALS PLAN

INCOME Goal for this MONTH:

Brainstorm how you could create it:

PRODUCT	PRICE	# SOLD	TOTAL

WHAT DO YOU NEED TO DO TO GET THERE?

- ☐
- ☐
- ☐
- ☐
- ☐
- ☐
- ☐

What DAILY HABITS would help?

HOW WILL YOU CELEBRATE WHEN YOU GET THERE?

- ☐
- ☐
- ☐
- ☐
- ☐
- ☐
- ☐
- ☐
- ☐

IT'S TIME TO REVIEW

OCTOBER

⭐ What goals did you achieve in October?	☑ What goals do you want to have in Nov?

❓ What do you need to do to make them happen?	💕 What self care do you wish to feel in Nov?

♥November♥ BUSINESS

GOALS PLAN

INCOME Goal for this MONTH:

What __DAILY HABITS__ would help?

Brainstorm how you could create it:

PRODUCT	PRICE	# SOLD	TOTAL

How will you CELEBRATE when you get tHERE?

WHAT DO YOU NEED TO DO TO GET tHERE?

- [ ] _____
- [ ] _____
- [ ] _____
- [ ] _____
- [ ] _____
- [ ] _____
- [ ] _____

- [ ] _____
- [ ] _____
- [ ] _____
- [ ] _____
- [ ] _____
- [ ] _____
- [ ] _____
- [ ] _____
- [ ] _____

IT'S TIME TO REVIEW
♥ NOVEMBER ♥

☆ What goals did you achieve in November?	☑ What goals do you want to have in Dec?

❓ What do you need to do to make them happen?	♥ What self care do you wish to feel in Dec?

DECEMBER ★ BUSINESS PLAN

GOALS

INCOME GOAL for this MONTH:

Brainstorm how you could create it:

PRODUCT	PRICE	# SOLD	TOTAL

What DAILY HABITS would help?

HOW WILL YOU CELEBRATE WHEN YOU GET THERE?

WHAT DO YOU NEED TO DO TO GET THERE?

- ☐
- ☐
- ☐
- ☐
- ☐
- ☐
- ☐
- ☐

- ☐
- ☐
- ☐
- ☐
- ☐
- ☐
- ☐
- ☐

IT'S TIME TO REVIEW
♥ DECEMBER ♥

☆ What goals did you achieve in December?

☑ What goals do you want to have in JAN?

？ What do you need to do to make them happen?

♥ What self care do you wish to feel in JAN?

★ TIME TO GET YOUR NEXT WORKBOOKS!

what to do when you FALL OFF the Goal Getter wagon!

(1.) FORGIVE YOURSELF! SOMETIMES WE GET BUSY. SOMETIMES WE FORGET. IT IS NATURAL + NORMAL TO BE HUMAN + MAKE MISTAKES!

↓

(2.) REVIEW YOUR GOALS. READ THROUGH THIS WORKBOOK AGAIN. WHAT GOALS COULD YOU ACHIEVE THIS MONTH?

↓

(3.) Go PUBLIC. TELL A FRIEND OR ACCOUNTABILITY BUDDY YOUR GOAL. ASK THEM TO HOLD YOU ACCOUNTABLE.

↓

(4.) Go Get YOUR GOAL! REMEMBER THAT MOMENTUM BUILDS MOMENTUM. EVERY LITTLE WIN BREEDS MORE WINS. YOU'VE GOT THIS! KEEP GOING!

About the Author:

Leonie Dawson is a best-selling author and serial entrepreneur. Over the past 20 years she has taught hundreds of thousands of gorgeous humans how to build wildly abundant businesses and embrace their creative gifts.

Leonie has been recognised for her business acumen as winner of Ausmumpreneur's Global Brand Award, Businesses Making A Difference Award & People's Choice Business Coach.

WEBSITE: www.LeonieDawson.com
PODCAST: Leonie Dawson Refuses To Be Categorised
ACADEMY: LeonieDawson.com/Academy

YOUR Next STEPS →

4 weeks behind-the-scenes e-course on how
I've built a multi-million dollar net worth

Want to stop IGNORING your ###
& start creating ABUNDANCE instead?

Want to see behind the scenes of exactly how I've created a multi-million dollar net worth?

Want to grow your own income and savings with joy and consciousness?

Join thousands of other gorgeous humans on this practical, inspiring and FUN four week journey to transform your financial destiny.

LEONIEDAWSON.COM/MONEY

40 ⭐
daYs to CREATE + SELL YouR E-CouRSe

ARe You READY to EARN MORe, teAch MORE & finally Get YouR e-course done?

Are you still messing about NOT getting your e-course done? Or are you not sure how to use the tech behind it? Or have you created an e-course but it's not getting the sales you want from it?

In the span of 40 days, you are going to get your e-course DONE. And master the tech like a pro. And start SELLING it like crazy.

This is accountability, tech + marketing advice on SPEED.

LEONIEDAWSON.COM/ECOURSE

It's time to STOP talking ABOut writing A Book... & FINISHING →it iN 40 DAYS iNsteAd...

Want to get your book written, finished and out in the world, doing what it's supposed to be doing?

★ helping the people it is meant to
★ giving you expert status
★ bringing you new clients & customers
★ giving you an extra income stream?

Learn the book writing + book marketing success secrets from and internationally best-selling author who has sold over a million dollars in books!

LEONIEDAWSON.COM/BOOK

Want to know exactly How to Sell MORE (OR ANY!) of Your thing?

Consider this program an essential business success building block. In order to succeed in business you MUST learn how to sell, and do it well.

Sales Star is my much-requested long-awaited sales training.

★ The sales checklists & templates I use in my own business

★ Behind the scenes in selling over $14m in 10 hours a week

★ Create powerful, magnetic sales pages that make you MORE $$$

★ Things to fix to INSTANTLY to start earning more.

Essential for new + mature business owners alike.

LEONIEDAWSON.COM/SELL

You **CAN** grow a prosperous, profitable biz without social media!

When people find out I took a two year sabbatical from social media & still made over $2 million in revenue, they immediately say: "Can you even DO that? I want to do that. But, I don't feel like I can."

This workshop gives you:

- ★ 150+ ways to market your business without social media
- ★ 42 reasons to consider leaving social media
- ★ Successful case studies of businesses who don't use social media
- ★ How to increase your profit & reduce your work hours if you do decide to stay on social media.

LEONIEDAWSON.COM/MARKETING

Are you ready to grow a beautifully abundant business & shining life? Join 5,000+ gorgeous humans in my Brilliant Biz & Life Academy!

★ Dozens of my incredibly powerful, popular programs

★ Group coaching & monthly guest experts

★ Done-for-you templates, resources & checklists!

Get everything you need to grow a shining life & Biz ... all at a WILDLY AFFORDABLE price!

LEONIEDAWSON.COM/ACADEMY

Made in the USA
Las Vegas, NV
21 November 2024